Painting Czeslawa Kwoka

Honoring Children of the Holocaust

D1558782

Paintings, Lori Schreiner

Poems, Theresa Senato Edwards

ISBN 978-1-936373-27-7

Painting Czeslawa Kwoka
Honoring Children of the Holocaust

First edition 2012

Dedication

To all the innocents who died in the Holocaust
and to all those who died trying to save them.

Table of Contents

Introduction

One Saturday in 2006, I was sitting in a cafe reading *The New York Daily News*, avoiding a critical paper that was due in a week. In the back of the newspaper was an article about Wilhelm Brasse, a Polish political prisoner who survived Auschwitz. Because he was a photographer before the war, Brasse was forced to work in the "Photo and Identification Department," methodically taking pictures of the concentration camp prisoners. Among these were biracial children, Jehovah Witnesses, Catholics, Gypsies, Poles, political dissenters, homosexuals, handicapped individuals, and, of course, Jews. According to the article, Brasse said the faces still haunted him, especially the children.

The article included a strip of photographs, an example of his work. The pictures were of Czeslawa Kwoka, a 14-year-old Polish Catholic girl who died at Auschwitz. She was positioned against a metal stand that held her head still. The contraption had moveable type to indicate place of origin and identification number.

The next day I went to my studio, taped the strip of photos to the wall and began painting Czeslawa. I used a palette of greys, reds, beige, burnt umber and olive green. My tools: a palette knife, ebony pencil, a stick, but mostly my fingertips to streak and blend and rub colors across the page. Her portrait emerged, facing me, small in a bulky striped tunic, hair tufts spiking out. Her number in grey and black and white. Her eyes, her bony chin, the hollows of her cheekbones, the scab on her lip, the red-orange fire and smoke wisping into the background sky.

I shared the paintings with Theresa, who had worked one summer as a data annotator at IBM on Steven Spielberg's Shoah project, annotating testimony of Holocaust survivors. She wrote the first poem, Painting Czeslawa Kwoka, in response to my paintings and Brasse's photos; our collaboration began.

We learned what we could about these children from the data preserved by the United States Holocaust Memorial Museum in Washington, DC, and the State Museum Auschwitz-Birkenau in Oświęcim, Poland. The rest we inferred from their faces and the stripes, triangles, numbers, and stars they wore. We could not find names or stories for all of them, but we believe they all perished.

I visited the United States Holocaust Memorial Museum while in the midst of this project. There was a photo of a naked child in a vat of ice water, a "medical" experiment. The Nazi doctor held his small body under the water. The boy, maybe seven, looked up, exhausted, trying to avoid the camera. He was slowly freezing to death while the doctor held him down. They took his picture to document his responses. His parents were gone; he was alone. I saw his face through frozen water and wondered if he was one of the little boys I painted. I knew he could have been.

The paintings and poems are now complete. We have added color to their cheeks and words to their mute deaths. We wanted to know what happened, to imagine the experience of these 17 innocents who had no one to tell, no one to share their terror, no mom or dad to fold them in their arms and tell them it would be ok.

We wanted to remind the world, which can never be reminded enough, that they once lived, that they had names, and that their lives are irreplaceable and sacred. We pray they might be given some small measure of peace, perhaps another moment of the life that was stolen from them.

—Lori Schreiner, LICSW, MFA

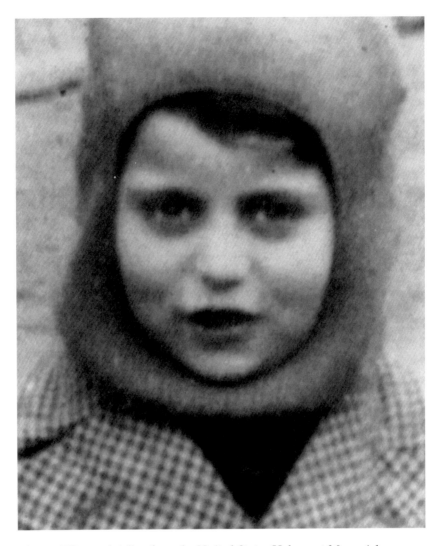

*Photo of Zigmond Adler, from the United States Holocaust Memorial
Museum, courtesy of Zigmond Adler's heirs, estate, and/or copyright holder
of this image. Locale: Liege, Belgium. Zigmond was born on July 18, 1936,
and was gassed at Auschwitz on May 21, 1944.*

Zigmond Adler

in a grey snapshot, you're a child in snow, dark, muted moons for eyes.
lungs clean before turning to the black dirt owned by Auschwitz.

in a color portrait, blue synthetic sky hugs your frozen face, your black eyes
drag us into oblivion. pupils, incessant whirlpools to a dank, vile place.

you're too young to know whose hand you clutch in dreams. the hand that
finds the blush of hope near your mouth, just under the cheekbone.

too young to understand why night erased your parents from your world, why
a concrete room strangles, children grabbing your flesh at the collar bone.

Photos of Gypsy girl from the archival collection of the State Museum Auschwitz-Birkenau in Oświęcim, Poland. Arrived in Auschwitz on October 10, 1943.

elegy for her

how is it we mourn for someone whom we didn't know?
to see three photos and wish her eyes transform?

to think about gender and how it shifts in each camera shot
her profile: a boy in a dress
hair jagged, chin cut as if there'd been a brawl,
empty fight with men gone very wrong.

her portrait: young girl,
eyes bent with sadness
stress around nostrils,
anger carved silent like glass.

her look beneath kerchief when asked
to shift her head right: young woman.
how is it her features soften against the force of chair
when dark cloth swaddles her hope of flowers,
river mist, laughter?

how is it that five numbers are all we have to find only three photos?
a "Z," *Zigeuner* (German for Gypsy) to create a category
in which they'll haul her out,
bludgeon any smiles she might have saved for someone
worth loving?

Photos of girl, who was the daughter of a German woman and a soldier in a black French garrison, from the United States Holocaust Memorial Museum, courtesy of Library of Congress. Germany, 1936.

Cameo, before

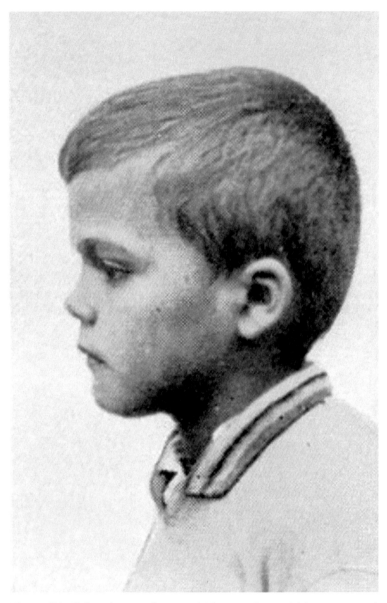

Photo of Rudi S., who was the son of Johannes S., an African man, and Anna S., a white German woman, from the United States Holocaust Memorial Museum, courtesy of Library of Congress. Germany, 1936. Rudi was brother to Ursula S.

Rudi's Profile

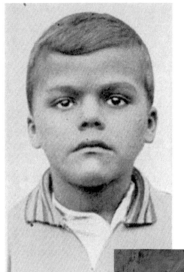

Photo of Rudi S., who was the son of Johannes S., an African man, and Anna S., a white German woman, from the United States Holocaust Memorial Museum, courtesy of Library of Congress. Germany, 1936. Rudi was brother to Ursula S.

Rudi,

Your eyes   your shields—
sting Nazi meanings.

Your mixture, fierce in color,
blends truth. Your flesh,
sand telling stories, shifts
around a mouth closed tight,
tongue locked inside,
stiff chin pink-blue
blackened "*Tragic*":
>   capital "*T*"
>   swoop of the lowercase "*g*"
>   dot of the "*i*" nearing
>   "*c*" barely there.

On tinted, textured canvas,
your broad face tweaks:
the shatter of nights
becomes globe,
black arcs, lines (—traceless
in black & white photo—)
guide roads for lost sisters
whose favorite color is you.

Your forehead, bruising sea
beneath mountain.
Purple rivers shape
the borders of your jaw.
I stand along the shores,
waiting for wind to spin
your mouth around.

Photo of Ursula S., who was the daughter of Johannes S., an African man, and Anna S., a white German woman, from the United States Holocaust Memorial Museum, courtesy of Library of Congress. Germany, 1936. Ursula was sister to Rudi S.

Ursula

Your dark eyes
distill
under a palette knife:
black rivers,
black pearls.

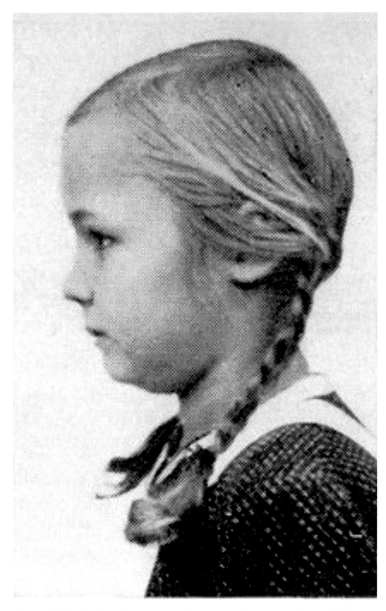

Photo of Ursula S., who was the daughter of Johannes S., an African man, and Anna S., a white German woman, from the United States Holocaust Memorial Museum, courtesy of Library of Congress. Germany, 1946. Ursula was sister to Rudi S.

Because of paint

I am clay
　　　　　molded
bruise beneath my hair
like a fig tossed around a mouth

my face
　　　　　a stagnant pond
yellow-green with algae
a blue hole
　　　　　tiny like a star
I slip into.

Photo of Emanuel (2 years) and Avram Rosenthal (5 years) wearing Jewish badges in the Kovno ghetto, taken shortly before their roundup in the March 1944 "Children's Action," when the Nazis raided the Kovno ghetto and removed all the children for execution. Photo from the United States Holocaust Memorial Museum, courtesy of Shraga Wainer. Locale: Kaunas, Lithuania, February 1, 1944. Photographed by George Kadish/Zvi Kadushin.

Emanuel and Avram Rosenthal, 1944

Shortly before their
death, little brothers
sit with stars.
Two- and five-year
hands curled tense
like crabs. Blunt
pain in each face,
like paper cuts.

Photos of Deliana Rademakers, Jehovah Witness, from the archival collection of the State Museum Auschwitz-Birkenau in Oświęcim, Poland. Deliana was born on February 24, 1923, deported to Auschwitz on November 30, 1942, and died there on December 10, 1942.

I will die at night

no. I try to speak

my voice cold as roots

I try to speak in camp

soldiers tug at stripes—what does   that   mean to me?
        mouth—lips—mouth—lips stripes, black/grey stripes   head
positioned like a relic   no,   I   try   to
speak

soldiers undress my soul, can you see it?   take it from me?

Jehovah holds my chin against a lightly tilted air.

I want to speak but will have no mouth, night catches voice, holds it till
morning.

I will die at night.   *Ik zal sterven's nachts*

I will

breathe slowly through shadows,   camera   flash   numbs

until I see again.   I want to move—

not   a   twItchlikedeath

not a fluff of hair.

Deliana

When I saw your painting in the studio, I saw scars   in colors   like
fruit. I felt scars, my fingers embedded in hardened edges of grief   you
came out in my palm. Light opened the paint, bringing you in—tasteless—
It wasn't right. There was nothing I could do. And before I left, you
burned yourself in me, scars in my hand like love.   I put you in my pant's
pocket when I walked, took you out to drive home. It wasn't right—I was
just a moving woman   helpless.

At home your painting   digital   corridors on your face   burns. I print
four close-ups to see what really happened   line them on the rug. I listen
to your mouth, fading   a black bird softening before his death flight. I
listen to your left eye wailing, black puncture wound to drop into after
hovering over your red cheek, its crevices melting. There is not enough
to tell me who you were, but I know your eyes scanned an iron-fenced
perimeter   thick metal crushing deep.

Now you are part of my life, your left eyebrow a fingerprint. Your face,
Braille touching my skin. I try to decipher the noise you carried on teenage
shoulders. Then   repetitions in my brain   the saying over and over again
of prayers. What else is there? Before I put photos, copies of your portrait
back in a blue folder, I balance nothing. There's no sense for balancing, only
space for my hands to stop tracing the valleys on your cheeks.

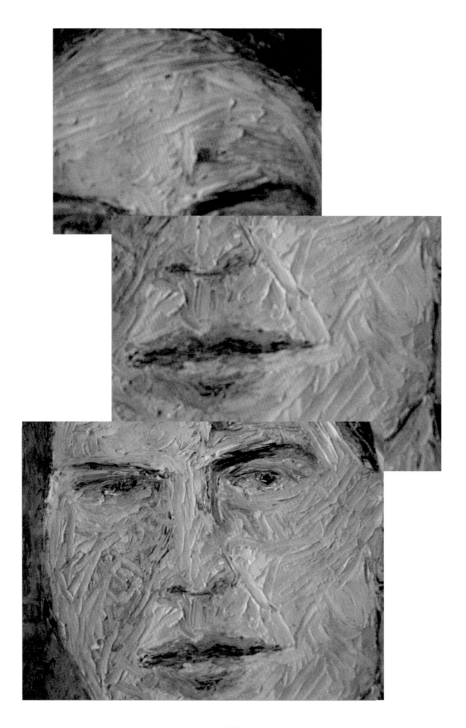

Soldier Boy

Time's obscure in paint:
your face / hair,
grey bones fallen from my father's wings.
Crystalline, they rest in your painting.
My father, a soldier alone in grey shades,
rustle left, gun ready, blood drains beneath his eyes.

The artist's paint is thick: your scalp
etched hard, my father's skin
emptying to shape your ear,
his time, black on your shoulders.

When they build your wings,
carve into young shoulder blades,
my father remembers he prayed for daughters.
She paints darker, each push of brown
fighting, your black eyes   trenches
those lonely holes of war.

Present / past amalgamate:
a dead man from clouds,
a boy alone, your cap edge,
blackened path of soldier bones,
dissolves in grey   slanting,
collar / era
tight around your neck.

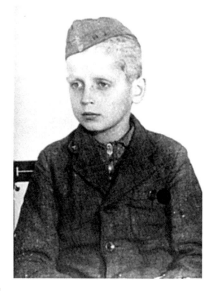

*Photo of child prisoner in the
Jugendshutzlager Litzmannstadt,
concentration camp for Polish
children, from the United States
Holocaust Memorial Museum,
courtesy of Instytut Pamieci
Narodowej. Lodz, Poland, 1943.*

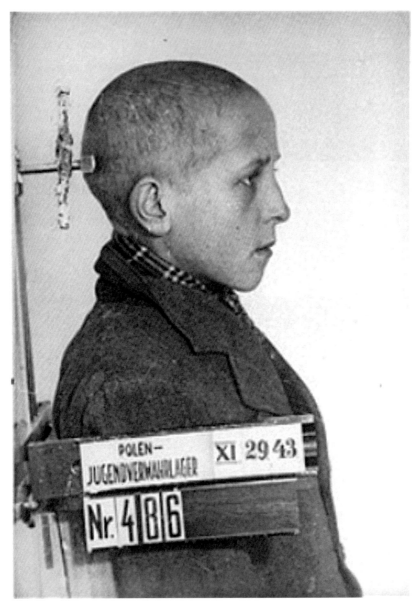

Photo of child prisoner in the Jugendshutzlager Litzmannstadt, concentration camp for Polish children, from the United States Holocaust Memorial Museum, courtesy of Instytut Pamieci Narodowej. Lodz, Poland, November 29, 1943.

Lost in Purple

Painting Czeslawa Kwoka

I

In Brasse's black and white photos,
you are a young girl with a round face
dropped into a flat, grey world,
26947 sewn on a striped wardrobe,
naked beneath these numbers.

What does color bring to you?
In color you move through our minds.

In color you are a movie star: Mia Farrow—
slightly protruding upper lip, swollen bottom
forms a dense shadow to your chin.

In color you are a young woman
bleeding from within: pale skin
filters red to pink. This is the
girl you are at Auschwitz, Czeslawa.

You are not a criminal.

*Photo of 14-year-old
Czeslawa Kwoka from the
archival collection of the
State Museum Auschwitz-
Birkenau in Oświęcim,
Poland. Photographed by
Wilhelm Brasse. Czeslawa
was a Polish Catholic, born
on August 15, 1928,
deported to Auschwitz on
December 13, 1942. She died
there on March 12, 1943.*

II

Your full color portrait
forces our reaction—
your hair is the warmest
fall in a dead winter, amber
background sparks the short, matted
bristles: adolescent questions
quickly extinguished when a scarf adds
texture, diagonal patterns, another
look of a 14-year-old prisoner.

In color you transform: we can
touch your swollen mouth, feel the
voice beneath the left side of your face,

where greys mix with pinks,
a rash of illness.

The contrast holds us.

III

In a soft color profile,
above and slightly right
of 26947, we see a tear
from your right eye spilling down,
just underneath skin transparent,
thin from a bleak setting.

We follow the contour of your
smeared mouth, slightly opened,
trace from lower lip to the
bottom of your chin:
this part of pinkish-grey flesh
appears as number 7.

This is not intentional.

IV

In color we feel the
blacks of uniformity,
harsh marks of suffering
blacken the scratched
shadows below your nostrils.

The black slit above your
grey lower lip sucks us
empty—your eyes, black
oval platters reflecting
SS soldiers and worse
within deep, grey carvings.

Black is blacker in color.

V

Painted close-up: a bright
yellow backdrop brightens
the scarf's pattern, your hair
hidden in black and white
becomes strands of sunlight,
movement on still life.

Yellows warm your cheeks,
your forehead clear of dirt,
yellows remove the dark patch
from the tip of your nose we see
in each of Brasse's photographs.
Yellows plunge orange,
settle on the center left of your chest.

You can breathe them in.

Photos of 14-year-old Czeslawa Kwoka from the archival collection of the State Museum Auschwitz-Birkenau in Oświęcim, Poland. Photographed by Wilhelm Brasse. Czeslawa was a Polish Catholic, born on August 15, 1928, deported to Auschwitz on December 13, 1942. She died there on March 12, 1943.

Suzanne's Smile

I try to understand why blue?
Why shades of little boys

juxtapose a china doll face
dressed up for synagogue.

Artist's decision trivial compared
to a two-year-old being arrested.

Hands clenched in white,
doll's arm fastened for safety.

You know only hand holding
towards a brick building your parents

pray silently in. Thoughts offered up
for their daughter's marble eyes,

bouncing hope above perfect chin,
teeth tiny, white Chiclets.

I remember these shapes, watching
my sons' little buds transform.

Growing pains soothed on teething rings,
cool washcloths, crib rails used for rubbing.

What kind of life has your little pulps
crushed before they really chew? What

can be said for oils and movement, artist's
own soothing: sealed grin beneath your nose.

Photo of Suzanne Carola Hochberr from the United States Holocaust Memorial Museum, courtesy of Robert Bahr. Locale: Amsterdam, The Netherlands, 1941. Suzanne was deported to Auschwitz on July 15, 1942, and killed there before she was three years old.

Photos of a Ukrainian political prisoner from the archival collection of the State Museum Auschwitz-Birkenau in Oświęcim, Poland.

Reasoning for a Ukrainian Boy

You remind me of Jeffrey, a boy I knew in school: large head,
level cheekbones, disproportionate lips, ears like giant thumbs pressing.

Jeffrey was an outlaw in the sixth grade.

What did that mean? Sitting in desks, middle school girls lift
legs when he walks around classrooms. Cooties through floor patterns,
souls. Outlaw effects.

You remind me of him, but looks skew: your hair like skin,
light eyes, lost ideas beneath striped hat / stripped Adam's apple,
anger. His dark hair greased, black eyes smiling, ridicule.

A skein dangles: Jeffrey's laughter, lips buckling, saliva thrown
across the room. It connects to you. forwhatreason—whatisthereason?
him classroom   comfort   juvenile   delinquent unscathed / you
political prisoner where children burn.

Invert triangle / five numbers / forwhatreason / thereasoniswhat? create
wardrobe / badges / ways to walk in fear because transparency stopped
exploding saws silent from your mouth.

Jeffrey was an outlaw in the sixth grade.

I try to level—
Reasoning's straight line crumbles in air.

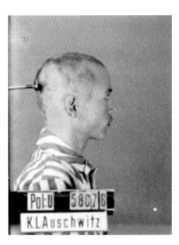

*Photo of a Ukrainian political
prisoner from the archival
collection of the State
Museum Auschwitz-Birkenau
in Oświęcim, Poland.*

Photo of a Ukrainian political prisoner from the archival collection of the State Museum Auschwitz-Birkenau in Oświęcim, Poland.

In these paintings

orange is beautiful,
a bright summer sun
warms skin

your head white putty,
metal wedged within

lavender aura, your
body escapes

geometry: red, restless form
your mind makes kite.

Elzbieta Konarska

First look at your photograph:

I see my friend who paints you. Ten years old, her hair like yours—cut at mid-ear, bangs give way to a girlish sweat that holds the head's shape. My friend who paints you sees the nape of neck secured to a cold steel clamp— a part of chair made by fear. Was this what my father saw when he put wood into his silver vise? That steel device, a toneless tuning fork, no ... a distorted metal hand pressing into a fragile valley on the back of a neck. Was this why he spent hours at his work bench, securing objects in metal claws connected to straightness? I think my friend who paints you has this same obsession with all things straight even though straightness can lean to one side, tilt farther away. No ... this is my obsession.

First look at your painting:

I climb the red and black ladder up your long grey neck. Cross the steady bridge over a chalky blue, slide down to linger at the earlobe. Your hair— black pouring rain—never lands, autumn ablaze along the hairline. Your face, a contrast from the photo: bright pinks, tans, slight undertow blue, a rush of life on your right cheek. My friend who paints you rubs the paint to form a speck of lavender mouth beneath a sculptured tip of pink. My friend

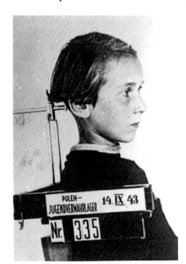

who paints you sees her mother's face, slight curve upward of the right nostril. She grips a stick to shape the girl with stars for eyes. In war my father prayed for girls. Under stars and saturation, he knew when he made it home, he'd never have boys. He's still as stars in a muddy sky.

Photo of Elzbieta Konarska, child prisoner in the Jugendschutzlager Litzmannstadt, concentration camp for Polish children, from the United States Holocaust Memorial Museum, courtesy of Instytut Pamieci Narodowej. Lodz, Poland, September 14, 1943.

Painting Czeslawa Kwoka

After days your painting

lies still on the floor.
the cat's body, paw touching
the tilt of your head
as if to reprimand

from afar
a blackened swan, your neck
to hold the sternness of chin,
lips scolding

Your photo

has sharp black angles of chair
your face,   soft tired wonder
held in place by cold perpendicular—
closer, my nose pressed to paper,

your face blurs,
white flatness
dark cartoon eyes
wait.

Today There's Lavender
(to Gad Beck)

Shadow under my left eye
A spring field
My look far
Not like that day
Our chests split
Lungs pounded in water
Clear as love

Soon, soon night's parade
Will march its fevered fantasy
Into your breath
A heat so calm
It followed me into death

There never was control
Just choices made
Now colors mixed
Made
A pink I never forget
Lights my face
Today there's lightning

Photo of Manfred Lewin, gay male and member of the Hehalutz Zionist youth movement, from the United States Holocaust Memorial Museum, courtesy of Jizchak Schwersenz. Berlin, Germany, 1941. Manfred was born on September 8, 1922 and was deported to Auschwitz in November 1942, where he perished.

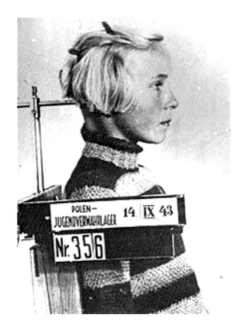

Photo of child prisoner in the Jugendschutzlager Litzmannstadt concentration camp for Polish children, from the United States Holocaust Memorial Museum, courtesy of Instytut Pamieci Narodowej. Lodz, Poland, September 14, 1943.

A Last Look

I wonder what Lori sees in black/white:
your face already dead? skeletal, cheekbone
distended into eye, swan neck like Elzbieta's.

What Lori feels through color, her fingertips
sweat, find new magenta highlights, mold pink
putty to protrude your lip like Czeslawa's.

With your photo comes beauty harnessed,
hair like a bouquet. Your painting a reminder:
porcelain, kiln fired, beauty as if figurine.

I wonder what is seen through young eyes tight
with fear: sodden dirt? ghosts? provisions children
play with, a last look, like prayer, past prejudice.

Photo Chaja Garbasz from the United States Holocaust Memorial Museum, courtesy of Shulamith Garbasz-Zimet. Poland, 1939. Chaja later perished in the Holocaust.

Chaja on a Summer Day

Acknowledgments

Grateful acknowledgment is made to the editors of the following literary journals in which the listed work or previous versions first appeared and/or were reprinted:

AdmitTwo: "Painting Czeslawa Kwoka" collaboration
Autumn Sky Poetry: "Painting Czeslawa Kwoka" collaboration reprint; "elegy for her" collaboration
BleakHouse Publishing: "A Last Look," "Deliana," and "Today There's Lavender" collaborations
elimae: "because of paint" collaboration
Trickhouse: "Zigmond Adler," "Elzbieta Konarska," "I will die at night," and republish of "because of paint" collaborations
"Painting Czeslawa Kwoka," poem only, is included in *Voices Through Skin* by Theresa Senato Edwards, Sibling Rivalry Press, 2011; *Poetry Super Highway* Open Poetry Reading, BlogTalkRadio, February 2009
"Painting Czeslawa Kwoka" collaboration was included in *Holly Rose Review*, February 2009, special addition to the PEACE Issue for Facebook, limited viewing; shown at Windham Art Gallery as part of Words & Images: A collaborative show of artists and writers, June 2007, Brattleboro, VT; shown at Exner Block Gallery as part of Words & Images: second showing, July 2007, Bellows Falls, VT.
"Painting Czeslawa Kwoka" collaboration was awarded the Tacenda Literary Award for Best Collaboration, BleakHouse Publishing, 2007.
"A Last Look" collaboration was awarded the Tacenda Literary Award for Best Collaboration, BleakHouse Publishing, 2010.

****

Much gratitude and acknowledgment is made to Caroline Waddell, photo archivist at the United States Holocaust Memorial Museum, and Wojciech Plosa, head of archive, the State Museum Auschwitz-Birkenau in Oświęcim, Poland, for their help in obtaining the rights to use these black and white, sepia photos with permission. A special thank you to Annmarie Lockhart, our publisher.

About the Artists

Lori Schreiner is a social worker, writer, and painter. Her writing has appeared in *The Best of Write Action* No. 1 and 2. Her paintings have been shown in New York City, The Windham Art Gallery, and other local venues in Vermont. In addition to her creative pursuits, Lori supervises the children's program at a community mental health clinic in Vermont and is currently a member of the Brattleboro West Arts Association.

Theresa Senato Edwards' first book of poems, *Voices Through Skin*, was published in June 2011 by Sibling Rivalry Press. Edwards teaches and tutors at Marist College, is scholar-facilitator for the New York Council for the Humanities' Conversations Bureau Program, is founder of *Holly Rose Review* (archived online), and blogs at TACSE *creations* (www.tacse.blogspot.com).

49024077R00034

Made in the USA
Middletown, DE
03 October 2017